Teenage Angst In My Twenties

Poems

Risa

Some of the material in this book has been
previously published in another format.

First Edition

Cover Designed by Carolina Altavilla

Edited by Eleana Norton

ISBN 978-8-218-69836-2 (pbk.)

For every version of me I've been, and every person who's ever felt too much, too soon, or too often.

Section 1: Workin' Girl

Workin' Girl

At Work.
Fuck.

It's A Me, Mario

You know life's getting hard when
you wish you could quit the job you just got
for the one you had before it.
Trying to level up but the whole world is
stacked against you.

Managing the Manager

Sometimes, (all the time)
I just want to punch you
in your bitch mouth.
Forever wishing your nametag didn't say
"Manager" on it.

Wannabe Carrie Bradshaw

There's some type of irony that comes from
feeling like a struggling artistic girlboss who's
just barely scraping by in the city,
But actually being a part time department store
worker while still living in your parents' house
and not paying a dime.
Not the twenties I imagined living but it's the
twenties I got.

Green Moose Guava Juice

You are the most vile woman I think I'll ever
know.
You can talk your talk, but I'd prefer you eat
crow.
Bushy blonde hair, big enough to hide your
secrets in.
In order to have a conversation, I'd need to
down a bottle of gin.
God has graced you by making you ten feet tall,
but I'm not afraid of you, or the way you look
down at us all.
That mauve lipstick you wear makes you look
like a vampire,
I still can't freaking believe I'm the one you
chose to hire.
Your flouncy customer service voice may have
corporate fooled,
but if any customer or employee were to vouch
for me, we'd have you overruled.

The best way to describe you is to say that you're icky,
I feel bad for anyone else named Vicki.

Just Walked Into the Office

I don't even think
the English language
has words that adequately express
how much I don't want to be here.

Shitting on Company Time

There is no space more underrated
than your favorite bathroom stall at work
in which you hide when times get tough.

Asking My Dad For Resume Pointers

Am I using
the right power verbs in my resume
or can you not
hear my desperation
when you read it?

It's the Retail Life for Me

We should normalize customer service workers saying "no."

Who's gonna tell the customers that we don't have the answers either?

The Customer is Always Right

If one more person comes through my line and
says,
"Oh iT MuSt Be FrEe ThEn,"
when their item doesn't scan,
"JuSt ThOuGhT I'd GiVe YoU sOmEtHiNg tO
Do,"
while throwing an item at me to fold,
"YeAh, A MiLLiOn DoLLaRs,"
when I ask if I can get them anything else
today, or
"WoW, IsN't It sO nIcE OuT,"
despite the fact that I'm working an eleven-
hour shift and any trace of daylight will go
unseen,
Just kill me.
Actually, don't even bother. Retail did that
already.

I Know You Relate to This

I've never had the near-unavoidable urge
to repeatedly slam my head into the table
until I started working here.

This is a Professional Corporate Environment

Who would've thought that one little email could get
so many different pairs of panties in a twist?

Mondays Are the Best Saturdays

Was graciously gifted
a plaque to keep in my bedroom
that says
"Dear weekend,
come back,
I'm not done with you yet."
But coming from someone who has worked
every single weekend
since I practically popped out the womb...

Weekend, I am SO fucking done with you.

Pulling Up to Work Like

Damn, I was really hoping I was going to pull
up into the parking lot to find
that the whole place went up in flames.

Section 2: General Angst

Teenage Angst in Your Twenties

Sometimes I just hate everything.

Covergirl

Sometimes life is easy, breezy, beautiful.
Sometimes I stab myself in the eye with a
mascara wand and
can't remember what it's like to want to be
alive.

Little Ditty

I used to think depression was the worst
feeling. But I was wrong.
It's nostalgia.
Feelings and memories that have me singing
John Mellancamp shit to myself.
Shit like first loves, late nights, and early life
lessons.
Like living broke, house parties, and driving
cars older than you were.
Like big dreams, fearing the future, bouts of
ambition.
Like small-town gossip, never sleeping,
blasting music out the open windows of your
ancient car just to feel something.
Hung on to high school as long as I could but
nothing good lasts forever.
I just thought I'd float instead of hitting rock
bottom.
I hope Jack and Diane fared better than I did.

Some Things Better Left Unsaid

We all wanted to do it.
Have sex too soon,
stay up til dawn,
drink til we couldn't tell which way was up.

But they didn't tell us that
sex is just a maneuver,
we'd be tired in the morning,
and living on autopilot is an addiction.
I wish there was someone to warn me.
Nothing lasts forever.

I Feel Elderly

Everything is different now.

I sold my Nissan and replaced it with a Mazda.
It's slower but more practical.

A new general store moved into the center of
town where the flower shop used to be. I had
never been to the flower shop, but that doesn't
mean it's not supposed to be there.

There used to be five of us, but now only three
of us show up to the Mexican restaurant to
reminisce about our high school days.

I used to let people tell me who I am, but now I
tell them how I feel. Verbatim.

Everyone always told me such good things
about growing up. But I just feel like I'm
missing something.

Maybe I'll Just Die Then

I'm always stuck between a rock, and a hard
place.
I want equal pay among the genders, but still
want you to buy me dinner.
I want to save the Earth, but I hate those
fucking paper straws.
I want people to tell me that I'm working hard,
but I don't actually want to work hard.
Maybe I'll just die then.

Your Own Worst Critic

I've got acne scars so deep that they won't go
away unless I surgically remove them.
Stretch marks so prolific they look like the
roots of a tree.
I have a big honkin' nose,
And fat little toes,
But I wouldn't think twice about any of these
things, if they weren't on me.
Why am I like this.

Pumpkin Spice

I've had palm readings done.
Restricted my diet down to rabbit food.
Woken up at the crack of dawn to meditate.
Paid two hundred dollars a month for someone
to tell me how to work out.
Exclusively gone to holistic doctors.
Searched extensively for signs in my birth chart
for proof that my virgo moon is the problem,
not my lifestyle.
My goal was to be "that girl," but instead I'm
more depressed than when I started.
Not even the healing crystals can save me now.

Mother Knows Best

I have a friend.
She's moonlight in human form.
Cool, mysterious, an otherworldly type of
beauty, inside and out.
For a long time I would've given anything to
look like her, be like her.

But one day I realized,
perhaps I'm not moonlight, but sunlight.
Warm, approachable, a tender type of
beautiful.
We are not the same, but both beautiful.

But that's not a new conclusion. That's
something your mother tells you in a fitting
room to make you feel better when the ugly
clothes don't fit.
So what do I know?

Blood Clot

All I know is blood.
The tattoo ink on my body bleeds into my
organs.
The pen I used to write this bled onto the
paper.
My lady bits bleed once a month.
The tears that I can never seem to hold back
bleed down my cheeks.
Anger bleeds into my words.
The heart that I wear so daringly on my sleeve
bleeds existentially.
All of this blood loss, and yet, every day, I rise.
There is no strength like the hold of a blood
clot.

Allergic

Sometimes,
when people call me pretty,
I remember that they call flowers pretty too,
until the flowers make them sneeze. Then all
bets are off.
You went from prime picking status to rotting
on the sidewalk.
For my own sake I hope I never make you
sneeze.

Tell Tale Heart

Usually, when people tell me I'm too sensitive,
I tell them in my head to shut up.
Never out loud, always in my head, because I'm
non-confrontational as well as sensitive.
It's not always a problem,
and in fact, most people would say it's one of
my finer qualities.
Until you try to get me to do something that's
supposed to be fun,
like going to see a movie.
You'll be sitting there perfectly content and
enjoying the show,
while I'm sitting right next to you and sobbing
into my popcorn because
"You just don't get it, the villain isn't inherently
evil, they're just misunderstood!"

God, I need to calm down.

Everything is as it Should Be

You went from being the extra friend walking
behind the other two on the sidewalk,
fantasizing about one snapping an ankle and
the other face-planting into the concrete,
to walking on the sidewalk all by your fucking
self.
Good on you.

Sober

My friends call me Marty.
They say it's short for Party Marty, my drunk alter-ego,
but they haven't called me Marisa in a while.
I wonder if they've forgotten what my real name is.
I wonder if they like Marty better.

I wonder if I like Marty better.

This Poem Reminds me of that Book I Read Whose Name I Can't Remember Now

Every year, to my dismay, late summer comes.
It rips my heart out and fries it on the BBQ.
Bops it around like a fucking beach ball.
I watch as the sun sets earlier and earlier and I
wait for the dread to set in.
It'll still be hot through September, but it's not
the same and everyone knows it.
Neighbors will start putting glass where their
screens used to be, locking up their homes and
cutting off the air supply without even knowing
they're doing it.
I won't hear the neighborhood kids outside
laughing when I come home anymore.

We'll start staying inside, and I'll have a lot more time to myself.
Time to think.
To think about last summer, and the summer before that, and the one before that.
It's like I'm drowning my heart in the ocean.
I think I might hate summer.

If Summer Were a Person, She'd Think I Don't Like Her

Summer is for atrocious tan lines, eating ice
cream for breakfast, and reading outside.
Or for driving with the windows down, star-
gazing, and going to sleep still feeling the ghost
of the ocean rocking.
My love of autumn distracts not from my love
of summer.
But as August ends and the autumn breeze
creeps in,
I'm reminded that everything eventually turns
to salt, anyway.

Sustainable Fashions

From Roisin Murphy's Ramalama

Unzip my body and take my heart out.
Embroider it on a sweater sleeve.
It is the most fashionable piece I own.
Wear it well.
Wear it proud.
The tears that accompany it, when worn
correctly, are my finest accessories.

Tug of War

A bisexual woman dating a man.
A woman, but a white one.
A depressed person, but a privileged one.
Someone who must be a voice for others,
but isn't always listened to herself.
Someone who is struggling day in and day out,
but who knows that so many have it so much
worse,
so even on a good day my heart is still

breaking,

    breaking,

        breaking.

Fuck a Pink Tax

"Are you a Coach girl or a Michael Kors girl?"
I think the real question should be who decided
that women don't deserve pockets?
Because I will find him, and I will kill him.
Only a man would decide something that
stupid.
I mean, shit, we barely have rights but now we
don't have pockets?

Can't Escape My Mind

They say your body is a temple.
I just wish mine came with a trap door.

Age of Adaline

Things get complicated when death is your biggest fear, yet you're so depressed you want to die.

Maybe I don't want to die. Perhaps, maybe, I want to live forever.

But in this misery? No, I couldn't live forever like this.

I think it might be scarier knowing that I'd have to live forever in the state I'm in.

This is 22

As a stone-cold introvert,
there is no better birthday gift,
than being left the fuck alone.

Birthday Gift From Hell

I have this mug.
It says, "When it rains, look for rainbows" on
the front.
Shut up, mug.

Goldilocks and the Three Bears

Living in New England, I get to experience all
four seasons.
It was always hard for me, as a child, to pick
my favorite.
But there's something about autumn.
Not too hot, not too cold.
And everything else around you is dying, so for
once,
you really feel like you're living.

Savers 30% Off Discount

Every night before I go to sleep, I pray.
I'm not really sure what I'm praying for at this
point, because happiness doesn't seem to cover
everything I want anymore.
Being sad for this long makes you forget that
material things won't fix all your problems.
Been sad for so long, it's almost uncomfortable
to feel anything else.
Maybe I'll go buy a new sweater anyway.
Can't hurt right?

The Other Side of Me

I never know how to feel when someone tells
me I'm "such a character."
Because I'm over here thinking I'm the Hannah
Montana of my own life but you probably only
see me as Miley.
And that's a reality that I'm not sure I can live
with.

Ramblings of the Mind

Silence is the loudest sound I ever heard,
tears are the strongest face wash I've ever used,
memories are the most addictive drugs I've
ever taken,
and loneliness is felt by so many that I often
wonder if lonely people are ever really alone.

Right Twix or Left Twix

Not getting a tattoo
is just as permanent as getting a tattoo.
Which life do you want to live?

Why do They Even Call it the Big Apple?

Everyone seems to be so inspired when they
come to New York.
And so I came, thinking I would be inspired
too.
But instead I saw grown men pissing in the
street,
crack whores on the train,
and literal hazardous waste puffing out of the
storm drains.
I was inspired alright—inspired to leave.
Alicia Keys got me fucked up talking about
some "these streets will make you feel brand
new."
I *feel* like I need to shower five times to wash
all the grime off.
The Broadway theater was small,
there were mice running rampant in the
museum,

and Central Park is just like any other park I've
been to, except with a hot dog stand.
I couldn't wait to get the fuck out of there.
They say it's a city of dreams,
but it's where my dreams went to die.

Bitchin' and Moanin'

Everyone says I bitch and moan too much.
Well I don't think they bitch and moan enough.

How's that for a complaint?

Probably Would've Complained About That Too Somehow

If complaining was a college major,
I think I still would've graduated late.

But I would've also still graduated with honors.

Nemo and an Anemone

Some people think my shitty attitude is
weighing me down.
I think my shitty attitude is in a perfect
symbiotic relationship with the rest of my
body.
I think wildly inappropriate thoughts at the
worst possible time and my body can't help but
laugh.
How else am I supposed to find joy in
anything?

I've Just Had Enough at This Point

Life is like a weighted blanket;
not heavy enough to take me out of my misery
but just enough to keep me down.

Pomegranate Seeds

I was told that if I starve myself my creativity will come back.

I was told that I only have to work this shitty job until I graduate college, when I can get a real job.

I was told that kids are mean, and everyone gets bullied.

I was told that I'll become more attractive eventually, I just have to grow into my looks.

I was told that my political opinion will be validated when I've gained some life experience.

What is it with this world and believing that you cannot be happy until you've been miserable enough to earn it?

Ten Thousand Spoons When All You Need is a Knife

Getting your dream job and staring at a blank computer screen.

Excitedly waiting for your brother to come home from school just to get in a fight with him.

Leaving the sprinklers on when it's raining outside.

Wanting one son, or one daughter, then bearing fraternal twins.

Gasping for air after working out and then choking on your water.

Jokingly asking if I hate you but I really fucking do.

Thinking nothing can touch you but you're allergic to gluten.

Thinking you're a good person but you're actually a male Pisces.

Giving your partner a kidney just for them to use it to cheat on you.
Calling your friend your "ride or die" but they take it too seriously and literally fucking die.
Getting a tattoo and hitting a bong despite the protests of your six-year-old self.
Spending all this time wishing you looked like the teenagers on TV then finding out the actors are twenty-five.

Buying a new phone just for no one to hit you up.
Joining a dating app to find somebody even though you hate everyone.
Going vegan unless they're serving chicken nuggies.
Writing all these poems just for no one to read them.

Too Much of a Good Thing

I love it when it rains.
But if it started to rain every day,
then I think I would find myself sitting here,
writing a poem that starts with
"I love it when the sun shines."

Terrible Twenties

You know how toddlers will do
some completely unimpressive thing,
like color outside the lines
or half-execute a somersault,
and you have to act impressed so you don't
hurt their feelings?
Well that's how my life is going.

If you couldn't guess, I'm the toddler.

Fast Times

Sometimes I think about
how many time capsules people have buried
and forgotten.

Every Man for Himself

I swear, if I have to eat "chicken, rice, and a vegetable" for dinner one more time—

No Damage Was Done in the Writing of This Book

I want to write pretty poetry.
Poetry with long, flowery rhetoric
that has a deeper meaning
and a clever title.
But my mind is sharp.
Not like a knife, but like a tongue.

So I write different poetry.
Poetry with simple words and
blunt messages
and titles that make no sense to anyone outside
of my head.
I may even hurt your feelings a little.
But you can trust me to give it to you straight.

No one gets out of this book unharmed.

Can't Bring You to the Beach, so I'll Bring the Beach to You

Sometimes the universe answers your pleas
faster than you expect.
I mean, just this morning I was walking out of
the grocery store,
thinking about how much I missed the beach,
while glaring cooly at the dirty snow littering
the ground.
And seemingly out of nowhere, a seagull
appeared,
and ever so kindly took a dump on my
windshield.

Not Everything is About You

I was driving home the other day,
and watched as a snowball fell from an
overarching tree,
and splattered on my windshield.

It felt a little too personal.

Again, Not Everything is About You

Egos are not just reserved for mean girls in movies,
or for the hockey team that you just met in that dingy fraternity basement.
Egos are also
hearing the line "you've got a heavy laugh for such a tiny girl," and believing that anyone who knows you would get an instant montage of you laughing in their minds whenever they hear that song.
It's believing that you're so chill that a rabid animal would sense your chillness and not attack you in the wild.
It's going to a public event and looking completely uninterested (even though you clearly bought tickets) and thinking the person you went to see will sense those same chill vibes and pick you out of the crowd.

It's telling your crush you hate them and expecting them to know that actually means you're completely infatuated with them. I'm a Leo, can't you tell?

Take This as a Sign to Heal

People are put in our lives to teach us a lesson.
You know you're a people pleaser when you
respond with
"Don't I owe you?"
instead of "Thank you"
when the lesson is learned, and it's the person's
divine time to leave.

Thanks, Dad

I don't always have to be right...

but I am.

Bullshit

And as if my day couldn't get any worse,
now I have a tummy ache.

No Mom, I'm Not Bitter. I'm a Realist.

There's nothing quite like waking up to the sound of birds chirping after a long, harsh winter.

I wish they would shut the fuck up.

Take What You Can Get

Self love is hard.

A lot of us expect to achieve it overnight.

But the first time I said "I love myself"

organically, and not by force while looking in

the mirror because some self-help book said it

would change my view of myself,

was when I remembered to bring a fork to work

for lunch.

Literally What the Fuck

I like to tell myself that
I don't care what people think of me.
But then I remember that
I wanted to paint my nails black,
but was too afraid that my parents were going
to think I "went goth,"
and so I settled for navy blue instead.

The Old Marisa Can't Come to the Phone Right Now...Why? 'Cuz She's Dead.

Ever since she died I've been living differently. I don't let dumb bitches control how I feel about myself.

My thoughts don't hold me back from accomplishing things that I could've done all along.

I've let pink into my life. And I wear bras as shirts.

I've grown a backbone; it's brittle, but it keeps my head on straight.

I'm not afraid of talking on the phone anymore.

I let people take pictures of me and don't give it a second thought when they post them.

I'm not afraid to ask questions at work, and I
write more than I ever have,
but most of all I've learned to grow from her
instead of pitying her.

I was the one who killed her, after all.

I Love The Library

There is something so beautiful
about a place where a bunch of people
gather together,
but are forced to shut the
fuck up.

It's Always About a J Name

It only LOOKS like everything is falling apart.
But it's not. Not really anyway.
If you want a friend that's going to tell you that
you're overreacting,
here I am.

I <3 Medium Ugly Men

Just because you think you're the ugliest
person in the room,
doesn't mean everyone else agrees with you.

Quite frankly, most people don't even care if
you are.

If the World was Ending, I'd Come Over

I'm definitely a "drive around the block to
finish the song" type of person.
But if somehow I time it wrong,
and we make it around the block but the song
is still going,
all I ask is that you sit in the driveway with me
while it ends.

Versatile or Just Politically Incorrect? You Decide

I am but an umbrella
that is used far more often to shield from the
sun
than to shield from the rain.

How'd You Know I Have Trauma?

Was it my "Songs My Dad Probably Likes" playlist?

The Ghost of English Teachers Past

Mrs. English Teacher —
AKA, the only person besides myself who has ever doubted me.

I've Seen Enough Honestly

Sometimes I focus so hard
that my eyes cross and
they just stay that way because
I'm too tired to uncross them,
too fucking tired, but
then I worry they'll get stuck that way
and so I sigh and I blink a couple times
and we're back in business.

Trying to Tell You How I Feel is Like...

The itsy bitsy spider trying its hardest to climb up your throat until the crushing rains of realization pour and wash it out again.

It's like trying to swallow a stubborn almond as it creates a shelf in your esophagus.

Or like trying to scream in the middle of a nightmare but no sound comes out.

Like the words are a giant fist and they're wrapped around your throat.

As if you're a toddler with strep and your throat's turned to gravel.

Like your tonsils swelling so big, one single word would cut off your air supply.

It's even like Marie Antoinette screaming a shrill "off with his head" and letting the guillotine chop the connection from your brain to your mouth straight off.

In other words, I just can't do it.

You've Invited Everything That Scares You to a Dinner Party...

But the guests might surprise you.

Because I'm not scared of taking the dream job that I feel unqualified to do. But I am scared of getting fired from said job when they find out I can't do it.

I'm not scared of the dark. I'm scared of what lies within it.

I'm not scared of telling you how I really feel. I'm scared of hearing you say that we're better off as friends.

I'm not scared of writing this book. I'm scared of what everyone will think of me after they've read it.

I'm not afraid of bugs. Actually, yes I'm afraid of bugs. They're definitely capable of more than we think they are. But back to the point. The

truth is,
the only real attendees at this dinner party
(besides the bugs) are your own thoughts.

And the fact is—

If you get out of your own head, you might just
surprise yourself.
If you sit with the dark long enough, your eyes
will adjust.
If they don't love you back, you'll still have
loved boldly.
If you never let them read the book,
you'll never hear them say how much they saw
themselves in it.

Give the bugs a seat at the table. Feed them so
they don't eat you first.

But everything else?

You'll realize all those monsters were just
mirrors. Take a plate; feed your soul.

Take This as a Sign to Put Your Fucking Phone Down

Yeah, the loneliness may get to you sometimes,
but what no one tells you is that
there's a certain freedom that comes
from knowing that no one is trying
to reach you.

Troubled Waters

When I say "you can't handle me,"
I don't mean you're unworthy.
I mean that dealing with me is like
scooping up water with your bare hands
and staring helplessly
as it falls through the cracks of your fingers.

Silent but Not Unresponsive

I peered up at the sky tonight,
as I do whenever I'm looking for answers.
But the silence I found,
marked by a starless sky,
was incredibly loud.

Make Like a Tree and Leaf

I yearn to be more like nature,
in that if there isn't a place for me,
I will simply forge one.
Much like the vines that I see
that have crept their way along
the telephone wire on my favorite street
on the way home from work.
They were not meant to grow there,
but nevertheless,
blossomed.

Truth

I wrote a poetry book because
I didn't have the skills to write anything else.
Not saying poets have no talent,
just that I don't.

Nobody Likes You When You're Twenty-Three

I've met twenty-two.
She's a raging alcoholic who somehow has both
the most inflated ego I've ever seen,
and the worst sense of self I've ever known.
But before her, I met nineteen.
Nineteen was hot shit. She was vivacious,
healthy, and so in love with life that you'd
never think she exists in the same body as
twenty-two.
But nineteen would never have existed without
sixteen. Sixteen was a walking contradiction.
She was terrified to dip her toe in the water but
as soon as she did, she spent the rest of sixteen
swimming.
But sixteen would be nothing without thirteen.
Thirteen taught sixteen that life was worth
living. It was thirteen who decided to take no

shit. That taking life by the balls was the only way.

Thirteen never would've decided that without first meeting ten, though. I feel bad for ten. Someone gave her the idea that she wasn't enough; and she believed them, until thirteen got involved.

But before ten was seven. Seven didn't have a clue what was coming. But she is, arguably, the foundation of it all. The Romantic, the Artist, the Kind; they were all born at seven.

I'm too old now to remember the girls who came before seven. But I do know for sure that they can't wait to meet twenty-three.

I haven't met twenty-three yet. But I hear that she's kind. That she's enough. That she takes no shit. She's quite the swimmer. Totally in love with life. And she's learned a whole lot from twenty-two.

Middle Fingers
Permanently Up

I get told a lot that I'm simply "too much."
I laugh too loud.
I tell people I've just met way too much about
myself.
I tell people I've known forever way too much
about myself.
I make people uncomfortable; apparently, I
can't just say to someone "you're going to be
my friend now" and expect them to want to be
my friend.

But notice how I'm always invited to events
where people need to break the ice.
Or how quickly I make friends.
Or how often I hear "you really helped me out
of my shell."

How easily I can figure out exactly who
someone is before they've even spoken a word.

So I'll continue to be too much.
I'll laugh louder than I ever have before.
I'll tell strangers my entire life story.
And tell my friends to fuck off if my entire life
story isn't something they want to hear.
And I'll continue to make friends by force.

I get told a lot that I'm simply too much.
But I also have a friend who always tells me not
to be afraid to take up space.
Because the thing about space is,
in this world,
you can never really take up too much of it.

Healing is Like

Screaming under water but without taking a
full breath first.
Clawing at your eyes enough to leave marks but
not enough to rip them out of their sockets.
Punching a bag but just not hitting hard
enough.
Eyes brimming with tears but not sobbing deep
enough.
Ripping your hair out but leaving chunks
behind.
Smashing a table but only one leg breaks.
Clenching your jaw but no teeth fall out.

Fuck.

Fuck!

Fuck fuck fuck FUCK.

Fuck fuck fuckity fuck fuck.

Fucking fuck.

FUuuuuuuuuUck.

Fuck.

That's all folks.

Nonsense Poem

I'm an anxious mess and
I'm falling apart but
I'd rather fall apart
than be ripped to shreds.
I don't feel pretty but
I do feel beautiful.
I don't think I'm all that smart but
I'm raw and I feel like that makes up for it.
I'm depressed but
I'm not sad and I feel like
that counts for something.

Gold Trim Pages

I don't know why I
save my prettiest notebooks
for final drafts when
the prettiest thoughts are the ones
I scribble messily in the margins before I
forget them.

The Bard

The thing about being a poet,
is that you spend half the time
writing,
and half the time
mourning the loss of ideas
that popped out of your head
just as quickly as they
popped into it.

Only the Good Die Young

I so badly want to write a memoir...
but I have hardly even lived.

Everything I Think Makes Me Cringe

I was going to start this poem off by saying
No OnE gEtS wHaT iT's LiKe To bE tHe StRoNg
OnE.
But I've never been "the strong one" so I couldn't
even tell you what it's like.
I'm the sensitive one.
The one who complains too much.
Who gives and gives and gives and then acts
surprised when people keep taking.
Who's worked in customer service way too long.
Who isn't asked how her day was when she walks in
the door anymore because someone's always
"wronged" her and people can't stand to hear about
it anymore.
Who sobs so hard people think she's laughing.
No one gets what it's like to be the sensitive one.
And thank God, because I wouldn't wish it on
anyone.

Section 3: The Heartbreak Diaries

Bambino

All I saw was yellow, in the beginning.
Sunshine, song birds, one happy family.
My whole world was wrapped up in you.
But you grew tired; perhaps I wrapped myself
up a little too tight and suffocated the heck out
of you.
And from there, that yellow turned to black.
The blinding dark, crows calling, all by my little
self.
I had nothing to wrap up in anymore. No one
to save me but me.
I suffocated myself the same way I suffocated
you, but I'll tell you what, I won't hold it
against me.

Monster House

I used to look at you and call you home.
But I have since moved out.
Now when I look at you, I see shattered stained
glass windows in your eyes;
a long-forgotten bird's nest, abandoned spring
after spring, in your hair;
vines creeping up your shoulders, no flower
buds but full of thorns;
creaky floorboards in your knees;
and the dust of a crumbling foundation at your
feet.
The light of a once-beautiful home dimmed,
remembered now only as the scariest house on
the street.
Legend says it's haunted.

Listen to Your Heart

How cruel is it
that one tiny organ makes such big decisions?
I begged and pleaded for it to let me love you
but every time, its answer was no.
Who is my heart to tell my mind no?

But then again, who am I not to listen?

Disney Princess Band-Aid

I never knew what it felt like to be heartbroken
until you broke me.
And it wasn't one clear cut down the middle,
no, but was instead shattered into a billion tiny
pieces.
Far too many to glue back together.
And too many of them turned to dust when
they hit the floor.
But I met someone.
Someone who, despite knowing he could never
put all those pieces back together, strung them
up as best he could and sealed them
temporarily with a bandage.
Because he knew that while he couldn't fix me,
he could do just enough to convince me that
some things are worth healing for.
And so I healed.
I put my heart back together and left no pieces
in your name.

Misery Loves Company

The same man who uttered the words "I love you, but I'm not in love with you," also couldn't utter the words "I'm breaking up with you." Funny how it's easier to break someone's heart if yours is also breaking.

Love with a Capital L

When I said I was in love with you,
I said it loudly.
I said it with arms outstretched,
soaking in the feeling the same way my skin
soaks up the sun.
So you can imagine how disappointed I was
when you said it back,
just as loudly,
but somehow sounding so much quieter.

Put it in Perspective

We had a lot of sex that summer.
The stickiest and sweatiest you can imagine.
Not because it was passionate,
but because it was summer.

Why Do You Linger

Even after you leave I still feel you on my skin.
The same way I feel sand between my toes,
an eyelash in my eye,
or the feeling of fleece fibers when they snag
your fingertips because your hands are too dry.
Perhaps I could just wash you off, but I'll never
forget how you felt.
Not even soap could remove that wretched
residue.

Did I Ever Really Know You

In the grand scheme of things, I only knew you
for a short time.
But knowing you is not the same as
remembering you.
Somehow, it's far less painful to think of the
one I know versus thinking of the one I knew.

Need Some Deodorant for How Much I'm Reeking of Desperation

I know you think of me every day.
I've never been more certain of anything in my life.

But do you think of me despite how things ended, or in spite of how things ended?

7 Things

Let's make a few things clear:
I didn't read Twilight for the plot.
I don't watch teen dramas for the character
development.
I don't wear makeup to impress you,
Or dresses to make you think I'm pretty.
I didn't get a rose tattoo to represent "self
love," I got it because I like fucking flowers.
And I sure as hell don't miss you.

But God, I just want to be adored.

This Sounds Like a Demi Lovato Number

I wish "I love you" was enough.
I wish that "I love you" conquered all, like the
books say it does,
and I wish that when we danced together on
that city terrace, it was out of love
and not out of apology.
I wish "I love you" was enough. But it's not.
We're hanging on by the thinnest thread and
using "I love you" as a Bandaid.
But someday soon the string will snap.
And "I love you" won't be enough to cushion
the fall.

Can You Believe I'm Still Writing Poems About This Shit?

I don't regret loving you.
In fact, I'm proud of the way I loved you.
I'm proud of how hard my heart can love.
I just wish it could know how it feels to love the right one as well as it knows how it feels to love the wrong one.

Rom-Com Without the Rom... or the Com

I have confused a life with you with a happy ending.
But the two are mutually exclusive.
When will I cease writing scripts for the way in
which my life should go, just for
no one to follow them? I stay up all night doing so.
There are so many things I deserve to hear.
Perhaps it's not a script I'm writing at all;
perhaps it's actually a laundry list of all the ways
you've wronged me.
If you had only said "I love you,"
maybe we'd be walking into a sunset right now,
~~Hand in hand,~~
~~Or through a flowery meadow,~~
~~Oooh or even driving a motorcycle~~

You know what,
I'm going to stop writing.

This Poem is Funny Because We Broke Up

People have been in love with me before.
I was afraid that it was something I would get used to,
and dare I say even bored of.
I had a friend say to me once that I don't date men; I make them fall in love. And that stuck with me.
But then you came along. And you love me because you love me, not because you feel obligated to love me.
All these years later, and I'm still not used to it.

When Adele Said "Never Mind I'll Find Someone Like You," I Didn't Feel That.

In fact, I actually want someone who is
absolutely nothing like you.
I want to turn to the page of our love story and
rip it out, clean.
No little page fragments in the binding, I want
it absolutely gone.

Gone like you are.

I will be plagued by your chapter no longer.
Gone are the tear-stained pages where the ink
ran.
I burned the pages that describe how our flame
died.

And I ripped out the ones that shattered my heart. So now they're gone.

Gone like you are.

I've started the re-write.
I found a much hotter love interest.
Mended the heart of the protagonist.
Fixed everything, from the tightness of the binding to the trees I chose to make the paper from.
It's quickly becoming a love story worth reading. And so it will stay.

Stay like you didn't.

Boys Don't Talk To Fat Girls

I never understood why my father would tell
me to stop eating even though I was still
hungry.
I didn't know that high top sneakers made my
legs look fat, and that's why my mom never let
me own a pair.
I never felt bad for wearing a bra in elementary
school, either, until my fourth-grade crush
pointed it out to everyone on the four-square
court one recess.
That's when I discovered that boys don't like
fat girls.

People made fun of me for re-wearing outfits in
middle school, but those were the only clothes
that fit.
No one understood why a sixth grader had to
be on a gluten-free diet.

My friends didn't know that I knew they were talking about me behind my back.
Boys talk to fat girls, but only so they can date their friends.

I thinned out by the time I got to high school but still felt like the same girl.
The only difference was how people treated me.
I found myself getting invited to things, wearing clothes that I liked, and making varsity sports teams...
And the boys, they talked to me now.

But then I got sick. And the medication's side-effects were weight gain, among other things.
I started hearing whisperings of people talking behind my back again. Asking my brother if I was pregnant.

When I went to college I lost weight again.
Boys lined up to take me on dates.

I fit in a medium for the first time in my life.
But I wasn't happy, so I transferred schools.
After all, there's more to life than the number on the scale.

I went to a school with my two best friends. Put some happy weight on.
And I met a boy.
And his first words to me were, "Hey, can I get your friend's number?"

It Takes Two

You know, I've had my vows written for you
since I was eighteen.
Not that it matters, because as I sit in my bed,
the pouring winter rain outside and my
pathetic feather lamp keeping my room just
light enough to keep me awake, we're not
getting married.
Not even close.
We did the whole strangers to friends to lovers
and back to strangers thing.
But now we're friends again.
And there I was, playing passenger princess
while you drove your car down the street, the
one that you picked me up in to take me for a
ride (because you know me too fucking well)
and I resisted the urge to tell you that I want
the cycle to repeat itself.
That I only ever want to be lovers, for the rest
of our lives.

But that's not the first time I've resisted the urge.

I resisted it later that same day, when you kindly drove my car to help me get my oil changed and we had to wait for 30 minutes.

When you looked into my eyes when you were talking to me; something I try to avoid letting you do because I have to resist the urge to rush to your mouth.

But due to how quickly you looked down, I wondered if you felt it too.

I resisted the urge to hold your hand above the table when we went out to dinner and you insisted on paying because you owed me for helping you with your English homework.

I resisted the urge when we first broke up but spent the whole night dancing with each other at our friend's birthday party.

And when we all crashed at a different friend's place on Halloween and you happened to fall asleep next to me.

So here I am shedding tears and praying harder than I ever have in my life that you'll find your way back to me.

Forever unable to resist the urge.

Love Your Own Damn Self

I don't miss you. Not really, anyway.
I miss getting flowers.
And love letters.
Having a reason to dress up.
Good morning texts.
Good night face times.
Always having someone to do things with.
Having a chauffeur.
Being someone's top priority.
Isn't it kind of strange,
how everything I miss about you actually has
nothing to do with you?

10 Things I Hate About You

I hate the way I cry whenever an old song of
yours comes on,
and the way I still feel the need to apologize.
I hate the way we used to fight,
I hate the way it took me so long to realize.
I hate that I haven't heard from you since,
but I'd hate it more if I had.
I hate the way that you've forced my growth,
and I hate how that makes me feel bad.
I hate the way that we could've been perfect,

I hate that I have to move on.
I hate that you couldn't get it together,
even worse is that I have to be strong.
I hate the way that I still care about you,
and the fact that I'm still your biggest fan,
but mostly I hate that I wish I could love you,
and I think... in another life... I can.

Tom's Diner

It is morning.
I stand in my kitchen in my
big t-shirt, whisking my eggs
and looking out the open window.
There was a storm last night,
so the air is cool and the ground
is littered with branches.
The sky is grey and the trees unmoving
but I can feel the chaotic energy
of another storm brewing.
Just how I like it.
I slice my vegetables and toss
them into my omelet.
I am thinking of you.
I sit down at the table to write
and all I can think is how
I left you because I felt lonely with you
but now I just feel lonelier.
It was never your fault.

Hurt

Sunlight streams through my
thin blinds but that's not
what wakes me.
I stir with tears in my eyes,
feeling around for a body
that no longer wakes up beside me.
I know I dream of you but I don't know
of what specifically.
Though I can probably guess.
I salivate at the sheer thought of you.
And your strong hands
running down my body.
Your raspy breathing in my ear.
Tongue on my neck.
If you were to ask if it's love or if it's lust
that I feel for you, I'd say that
it's not that I never loved you,
or that I don't now,
it's just that we're one in the same and
I've never loved what I see in the mirror.

Falling in Love is a Trap

Following my most recent heartbreak,
it occurred to me that I shouldn't settle this
time.
Compromise is inevitable, but
mistreatment is not an option.
And thus I began the journey to find my "next."
But I wasn't quite sure what I needed, so I
asked The Greats.

Romeo and Juliet said the most important
thing is devotion.
Bonnie and Clyde said it was loyalty.
Hades and Persephone said it was admiration.

Cleopatra and Mark Anthony said you'll just
know.
Paris and Helen said it was attraction.
Paolo and Francessca said it was care.

Edward and Bella said it was authenticity.
Jack and Rose said it was understanding.
Lancelot and Guinevere said it was fate.

But the thing about The Greats is that all their stories
conclude that true love can't help but end in tragedy.
True love doesn't have a plan. You can't go searching for it.
But you can bet that when you put your heart on the line,
tragedy follows.

Jaded

I'm grateful to the sky because
I would've felt so much more alone
sobbing in the car today
had the sky not been sobbing with me.

It's ironic that my therapy is
screaming the lyrics to every sad song
that comes on the radio while I drive
when you used to hate how I'd sing in the car.

I appreciate the sky's constant support though
I fear that I'm the reason for this
uncharacteristic monsoon season.

Did you ever even like me at all?
Every time I cry about you I think
it will be the last time.
But it never is.

It just never is.

Section 4: Maybe There's a Little Bit of Hope After All

I Got Another Match.Com Email Today...

We become so obsessed with the idea of finding somebody,
that we forget that somebody and anybody are not the same.

You deserve more than just anybody.

Tiny Stranger

Was sitting in my bathroom, peeing, as one
does, when an ant crawled through the gap
between the door and the floor.
Don't you know the bad day we've just seen
little ant?
Why would you choose this house to invade,
little friend?
The only crumbs you'll find on this floor are
bitter.
But it was nice not to be alone.

Team Edward or Team Jacob?

My mom always said it was bad juju to live on a dead-end road. That all the energy from the street in front of it literally stops dead.
But I think it might be nice to be calm for a while.
Raise a family in no-man's land.
See what the world is like when things aren't forced to be something, but can just be.

Teeth are Just Bones

My father always says, "Smile, and the whole
world smiles with you."
And so every time I'm upset, I smile at the
world.
Oftentimes, the world bears its teeth back at
me,
not in a smile but in a grimace.
Despite my father's best efforts, he couldn't
force the world to be kind to me.
But I learned that there's always something to
smile about.

Scar Tissue

I've always loved the feeling I get
when I go to the beach and look out at the
horizon,
like the edge of the world is right there.
It's a most chaotic place to be, on the edge,
but no other place keeps me quite as grounded.

Don't Open Your Umbrella Indoors

Everyone says, "It is what it is."
But I'm not falling for that.
Life will spit on you,
and call it rain.
You can either open your umbrella or fucking
dance in it.

Def (or Eventually Deaf) Leppard

There's nothing like
getting out of work after a long day,
mid-summer,
barreling down the highway at ninety miles an
hour, the wind nearly suffocating you because
all the windows and the sunroof are wide open
in your shitbox,
and you finally get to let out that pent-up
scream you've been keeping in all day, battling
the music streaming from your speakers.
The sunset's coming closer and your rage is
being left in the rearview.
Man, there's nothing like being a kid.

Cramp in my Side

It's not about being happy all the time.
You're not going to be happy all the time.
It's about continuing to chase joy,
and to never stop running, even when you
think you're out of breath.

Rupi

I wish I could hold happiness in my hand, just
to be sure it's real.
Wish I could build it on my own, so as to never
run out.
But, I guess, we make happiness every day.
Whether it's
Constructed,
Welded,
Folded,
Mended,
Deep-fried,
Sung along to,
Worn,
Torn,
Or even born.
Whether it's
Hidden,
Spoken,
Written,

Or even sometimes forgotten.

Happiness may fade,

and we may have a hard time building it,

but that doesn't mean it isn't there.

Coldplay Wrote "Yellow" After Meeting My Mom

My mom asked me to write a poem about her.
So I did.
And it sucked.
It ended up being this tacky little number about
how she's not just my mom, but also my
adventure buddy, my sounding board, my five-
dollar-ticket-Tuesday movie partner... you get
the idea.
But she's more than that. And deserves better.
But I couldn't figure out how to say what I had
to say, so the previous sorry excuse for a poem
almost made the cut. And then a song came on
the radio.
It said, "For you I'd bleed myself dry."
And I couldn't help but think how wonderful it
must be to feel that way about someone.
And then mom popped into my head. And I
knew what I had to do.

So, Darl, this one's for you:

If I'm going to write about Darlene, the word "mom" just isn't going to cut it. She's a lot more than that.

She's my adventure buddy.

My five-dollar-ticket-Tuesday movie partner.

The one who convinced me to drive an hour to some hippie's house to save a baby bird who had a broken wing because natural selection wasn't an option.

The one who picked up a random stranger on the side of the road one New Year's Eve, despite my protests, because it was below freezing and he didn't have a jacket.

The one who stole tiki torches off a random person's property and persuaded me to help her.

The only one who would open her sunroof while it's raining and scream the words to our song because it has the word "rain" in it and we had to match the vibe.

For you, mumma, I'd bleed myself dry.

I Guess Someone Really Does Listen to Me Count My Blessings

And it's funny because
you're everything I always asked for but
nothing like what I expected.

Silver Lining

Say what you will about my exes,
but I couldn't have asked for
better men to break my heart.

If You Were to Dissect My Heart...

And you stuck it under a telescope,
zoomed in on its veins,
and looked real close,

you'd see your name in every one of my blood
cells.

Mrs.

"I miss your body,
I miss you being around,
I miss you."
How lucky am I to have found a man that loves
my body, heart, and soul all at once?

Fall in Love with the Eyes, Fall in Love With the Man

His eyes are blue.
Not that it matters though.
When describing "my type" I never
felt the need to specify an eye color.
I specify things like intelligence,
or romantics or humor.
He just happens to have it all. Along with
blue eyes.
Blue eyes that are sometimes greener,
sometimes grayer.
Blue eyes, that do, in a cliche way,
glitter like the ocean.
The exact same blue eyes that I see
in all the childhood pictures hung up in his
mother's house.
The same blue eyes that crinkle when he
laughs,
and droop when he cries,

and the same blue eyes that
answer all my questions before his lips do.

His eyes are blue.
Not that it matters though.
I would've fallen in love with them regardless.

The Stairway to Heaven Ascends from the Bowladrome

As a child I was never afraid of thunderstorms.
In fact, I always quite liked them.
My mother used to say that thunderstorms
were just the angels going bowling.
Well there was a particularly rowdy game
playing last night,
and God, being the nice guy that he is,
woke me up so I could listen to them play.

I took the elevator on up to Heaven,
as the Stairway is way too long.
And when I arrived,
I was surprised to find,
just how similar the bowladrome looks
to the one in my hometown.

The same ten lanes,

with the same flickering lights,

and the same tattered shoes.

Even the holes in the floor were the same.

I grabbed a cup of popcorn from the machine

in the back.

It tasted like you.

Who would've thought that so much of Heaven

stays the same?

Someone Once Told Me I Look At You Like I'm In Love With You. I Am.

You're the only person I've ever been unable to read.
All these years later and my eyes still skim your pages but
come up astray.
And then I tried writing about you; and sat here until my brain started to bleed.

But I do know that I sink into those cornflower eyes like you would a beanbag chair.
That the magnetic pull from my hand to yours is strong but must remain ignored.
That you're the only person in the entire universe that with my life I want to share.
That every time I'm going somewhere I know you'll be, my heart soars.

I know that you're the only person that I'd stay
up till 1am to talk to.
That you're the one who makes me smile most.
That I'd give anything to spend a day with you.
That if you ever took me out, the whole world
would hear me boast.

I know that, from what I can tell anyway, we're
of one mind.
That when I'm with you, I instantly feel lighter.
That in a room full of anyone I've ever loved,
it's you I'd want to find.
That every day that goes by, my flame for you
burns a hundred times brighter.

I still cannot read you. I fear I never will.
And honestly, I've never been a fan of mystery
books.
But any book with your name in the title is
worth reading still.

Hear Me Roar

I like to write because it immortalizes my
current state.
Writing used to scare me, because I was afraid
of coming face to face with my raw being.
She's naked and afraid but boy is she mighty.
I used to hate her, but now when she screams
at the world I scream with her instead of at her.

You Shine All On Your Own

There was exactly one star in the sky tonight.
And no, I didn't mistake it for a plane.
I checked. Multiple times.
It was a perfect star.
I could see all five points, almost as if I drew it
myself.
It was big and bright,
practically begging me to pluck it from the sky
and cup it in my palm.
You know, for safekeeping.
But quite frankly I could never.
Not because I couldn't reach it,
but because I would never want to be the thing
that
dims its light.

Like Two Drunk Chicks in the Restaurant Bathroom

I looked at the moon
and then I looked closer
at the craters in her skin
and I told her that they're beautiful
and she smiled and
said the same thing about mine.

Weight of a Thousand Suns

I have all these things to say,
but not the words to say them.
I'm not lacking in courage;
people are free to know
whatever they wish about me.
What I lack is proper form.
It is not enough to say "I miss you" anymore;
not when, in reality,
my heart shatters to bits every morning I wake
up without you,
tears well in my eyes upon your voice
answering the phone,
my body aches with the wanting,
and my head splits in two while working
double-time to protect my heart,
on the off chance that you decide you
don't want this as badly as I do.
Not when
you've become my entire artistic muse,

I've practically written wedding vows in
between
my lines of poetry,
changed your middle name in my head from
"Robert" to "Forever,"
and spend every free moment begging
the cosmos to give us a chance.
I miss you.
But those words aren't enough.
Know that when I say them, they aren't empty;
they're carrying a weight so heavy
that even the sun cowers in fear.

Inspiration Chooses YOU

Every time I think
I couldn't possibly find any more inspiration
from the rain,
another drizzle comes,
and suddenly my pen
returns to my hand.

Acknowledgments

The biggest thank you goes to my family — for enduring years of my endless complaints and for surviving the relentless grammar corrections. Honestly, I don't know how you made it through, but here we are.

Next, a shoutout to teachers — because teachers matter. To those who doubted me, well, HA HA HA. And to the fierce few who believed I could, thank you for fueling the fire that kept me going.

A seemingly random but heartfelt thanks to Sam Pink. Sam, you don't know me, and honestly, I'm not even sure if that's your real name, but *99 Poems to Cure Whatever's Wrong With You or Create The Problems You Need* changed my life in ways I'm still unpacking.

And finally, to Max — partly for starring in a few of these poems yourself, but mostly for ordering that very book on Amazon with zero explanation. There was no rhyme or reason, but I'm convinced we witnessed a bit of divine intervention that day. Before that, writing a book wasn't even on my radar.

About The Author

Marisa Fertitta is a poet and emerging novelist who writes about love, heartbreak, nostalgia, feminism, nature, and all the messy metaphors life throws her way. Since publishing her debut collection, *Teenage Angst In My Twenties*, she's been busy sharpening her pen (and her wit) on social media and small-press anthologies. With a degree in Communications & Professional Writing, Marisa is currently juggling words for her first novel — and probably talking to ants, because why not make friends with the tiny strangers in life's bathroom moments?